FLORIDA INDIANS:
Noble Redmen of the South

Second Printing
ISBN: 0-912760-19-2
Library of Congress Catalog Card Number: 76-601

PUBLISHED BY

FLORIDA INDIANS: Noble Redmen of the South

By
EDITH RIDENOUR LAWSON

With Illustrations By
MIKE SKEGGS

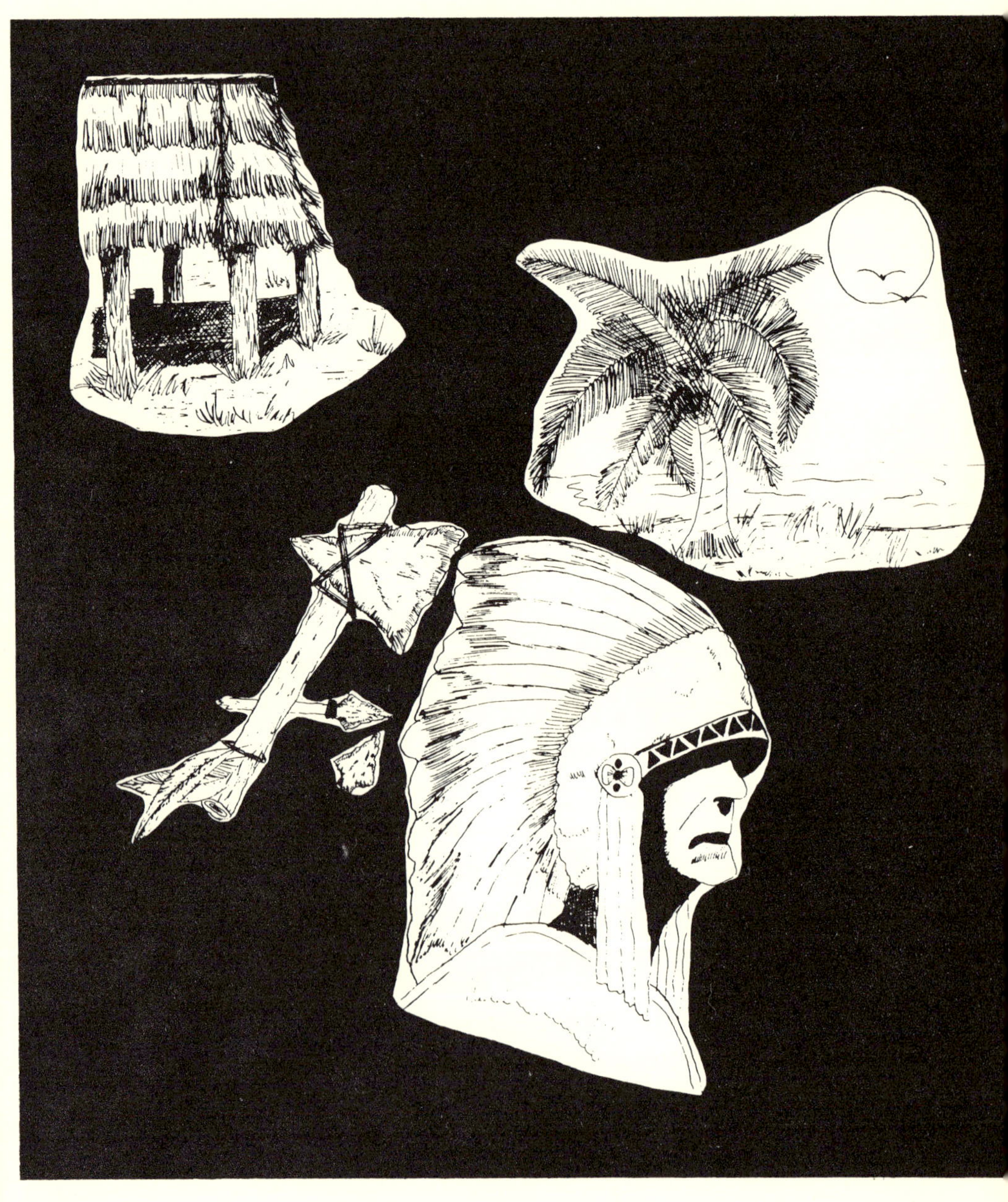

From an early poem on Florida:

"Have you not hard of floryda,
A coontre far bewest,
Where savage pepell planted are
By nature and by hest,
Who in the mold
Fynd glysterynge gold
And yt for tryfels sell?
with hy!"

(Note: *An Early Poem on Florida* was published in the Historical Society Quarterly July 1928, Vol. VII – pages 72, 73, 74. It is pictured there in the original writing. This earliest known poem about Florida consists of seven stanzas. Edgar Legare Pennington and Clark Sutherland Northrup explain that it was found in Bodleian Library, Oxford in Ashmolean Manuse 48ff 140b, 141 a poem on Florida (penmanship suggests early part of 17th century).

Of the seven stanzas the second refers to Florida, and is the one used here. It was printed by C. H. Firth in his *American Garland,* Oxford 1915. The same had already been printed by Thomas Wright in *Songs and Ballads, Chiefly of the Reign of Philip and Mary* (Roxburghe Club, 1860, page 213).)

"Indians were and are neither ignorant and bloodthirsty savages, nor misunderstood heroes. Indians are human beings like ourselves, living interesting normal lives in accordance with customs and beliefs which are prehistoric in origin — but greatly modified by several hundred years of contact with white people."

Bureau of Indian Affairs
Department of the Interior

Chapter 1

Space ships are often called birds by the men who work with them. An astronaut on his first flight in a space bird might begin his trip at Cape Kennedy Space Center, which is on the east coast of Florida. As he soars aloft out over the Atlantic Ocean, he can view the whole peninsula of Florida. If he looks closely, he will quickly understand why it is called the Land of the Sun or the Sunshine State.

Before he flies too high, he can easily pick out the most common trees – the oak, palm, pine, mangrove, and cypress. He can see the magnolia, royal poinciana, jacaranda, and countless flowering trees as well as the 30,000 or more named lakes that dot the land.

He'll get a glimpse of the St. Johns, largest of Florida rivers; the Suwannee, made famous in song by Stephen Foster; and the Withlacoochie, troubled by Indian skirmishes in war.

He may recognize the Peace River, known for its 'bone valley'; the Kissimmee, marked by cattle country; and the Apalachicola, remembered as a trade route before highways and railroads were built. He'll see others which furnish transportation and help for all living creatures of the peninsula.

No part of Florida is far from water. He'll see the longest coast line of any state except Alaska. The bays, coves, inlets, and islands make it look fringed and irregular. He can tell that there would be enough room to put the states of Connecticut, Rhode Island, New Hampshire, Vermont, and Maine inside its boundaries.

Georgia and Alabama lie to the north and on all the other

sides, he'll see water. There'll be the blue of the Atlantic Ocean, the Straits of Florida, the Gulf of Mexico, and part of the Perdido River, which separates Florida from Alabama.

Among the northern hills he'll see the white and shining buildings of the state capitol, Tallahassee, the pecan groves, the tung orchards, the oak and pine forests, and the rich agricultural land where once great plantations flourished. Long before plantations were ever thought of in that part of Florida, powerful Timucuan and Apalachee tribes built their villages and played their reed flutes. Some of their children learned to read and write. Some older Indians went to church dressed in clothes like those worn in Europe.

In middle Florida he'll recognize grove after grove of oranges, fragrant with waxy white blossoms and golden fruit. The prairies and ranges will mark the dairy and beef section where hundreds of cattle graze.

South of this he'll see Lake Okeechobee, second largest body of fresh water lying wholly within the United States. Around it he'll see fields of sugar cane which will help to satisfy the needs of many a sweet tooth for sugar and molasses. Nearby in the rich muck lands he'll see truck farms where mile-long rows of vegetables grow to be harvested and shipped to northern markets.

In the far south he'll see the broad "river of grass." It is the Everglades – widest, shallowest river in America, where Seminole Indians live on higher ground.

He may have to make a second or third trip skyward before he sees all this, but it's there and much, much more.

Chapter 2

If an astronaut could have looked down from a space bird upon Florida 15,000 years ago, he would have seen a population explosion. The ancient animals formed a multitude of both great and small as may never be found in one region again.

In that long ago time, the Bering Straits land bridge connected Siberia and Alaska. The narrowest part was at least 1,000 miles wide. Animals moved back and forth across that isthmus between Asia and America. Some of the large ones were giant elk, musk-ox, mastodon, elephant-sized ground sloth, saber-tooth tiger, camel, giant bison, and mammoth.

During the Ice Age, snow and sleet covered much of Canada and part of the United States. This did not melt for thousands of years. It destroyed plants and drove animals before it in their efforts to escape the terrible cold.

Alaska was pretty well glacier-free. Dry winds out of Siberia prevented much snowfall. Mammoths, deer, and other grazing animals perhaps followed grassy plains in western Canada and the great river valleys farther and farther south to escape the frigid cold until they reached the peninsula of Florida.

After a time, even here they suffered from cold, from crowding, and probably from diseases, as well as from the meat-eaters. The saber-tooth tigers, wolves, lions, and giant pigs followed and destroyed the grass eaters.

In these very ancient times animals and plants kept early man from starving and freezing. Everybody in the world lived by hunting, fishing, or gathering wild plants.

People knew how to make fire. Weapons and tools were chipped from stones, then used to kill animals. The skins or fur provided warmth, and the meat satisfied hunger. Many people lived in shelters made of brush.

People didn't hurry. As long as they had plenty of food, shelter, clothing, and no close enemies, they were content to live in one place. It took thousands of years for men to reach Florida.

Chapter 3

About 25,000 years ago a small group of hungry hunters must have been the first people to follow the animals from Siberia. Perhaps there were not more than a few dozen altogether. They wouldn't have had any reason to travel all the way to Florida, because there were animals in Alaska and river valleys free from ice.

But – thousands of years later many changes had taken place. The great, great, great, great, great and several more great grandsons of these hunters had to work harder to get food. They traveled as far away as Florida to get it when animals began to get scarce in the north.

The first hunters had no dogs to help. They depended on crude stone weapons, clumsy tools, and courage. The enormous mammoth was a favorite animal. One mammoth yielded enough meat to satisfy a small band of people for a long time.

Hunting is hard work. A hungry Eskimo hunter can eat from six to ten pounds of meat without stopping. Prehistoric man must have hunted mainly because he was hungry.

Why these first land-bridge visitors to America came, we do not know. Hunger, war, curiosity, or desire to explore may have forced them out of Siberia. Their coming could have been an accident. The true story of their experiences is lost in the past.

As the ice melted slowly over a long period of years, the sea covered the land bridge. Hunters walked across the ice in winter or used crude rafts or skin boats to cross over open water in summer.

Today the old land bridge is under a hundred or more feet of water. Fifty-six miles of water known as Bering Strait separate

Siberia from Alaska. The Strait may be wide and deep but this does not discourage modern bridge builders. Engineers are dreaming of building a bridge across Bering Strait to connect Alaska with Siberia once more if all countries agree.

Nothing seemed to stop prehistoric hunters in small bands from leaving Siberia and entering Alaska. As more came, the ancient animals disappeared slowly, usually one species at a time. Starvation, disease, climate, volcanoes, or hunters may have brought about this change.

Our world never stops changing. In Florida man has changed the natural environment so much over the past 150 years that many animals keep slowly disappearing today.

Some of them are found only in parks or zoos. Once the limpkin lived in great numbers in the Everglades. This bird cries only at night like a lost frightened child. Since the Everglades are being drained, the limpkin is fast disappearing because its food, a special kind of snail, is also disappearing.

The same thing is happening to the kite, since it eats snails that depend on fresh water. The roseate spoonbill, the scarlet flamingo, the sea cow or manatee, the alligator, as well as many more, suffer too from the changing environment.

In early days, when the big animals became scarce, some people fished, hunted small animals, and moved camp when the supply of food was gone. Others began to look for new ways to get food for themselves. By accident or through experiment some learned to farm.

Mike Skeggs

Chapter 4

A group of Stone Age farmers who lived in villages finally made their way to Florida. They farmed, made pottery, and built mounds. Their villages were always located near good farm land.

The women grew such crops as corn, beans, squashes, and pumpkins. All the work was done by hand, with wooden digging sticks, stone hoes, animal shoulder blades, or shells tied to wooden handles.

Florida became the home of people who built mounds. They were called Mound-Building Indians. The best history books that describe the culture of Mound-Building Indians are the mounds themselves.

Mounds were built in various shapes and sizes to meet the needs of the people. Some were large, some were middle-sized, and some were small. They were shaped like rectangles, squares, or circles. The land was naturally flat but was changed in some sections by mounds into a country of low hills. Most mounds were from ten to forty feet high.

Men and women worked together to construct a mound. Indians used hand-woven palm frond baskets to carry dirt and sand to the site. Workers used an earth ramp or steps as the mound grew higher.

The favorite seemed to be a temple mound. It was built in the form of a square or rectangle by using alternate layers of sand and shell. Sometimes clay was smoothed on the outside like frosting on a cake. When the mound was high enough, a temple was built on this flat base.

To build a temple, first a wooden frame was set up. This was covered with matting, thatch, woven reeds, palmetto, or whatever material was easy to get. Sometimes inside walls were covered with smooth clay. Here, all kinds of carved stone or wood ceremonial objects were kept. A sacred fire burned all year long in some temples.

Certain tribes built burial mounds. Some burial mounds contained great numbers of skeletons. In one mound on the west coast of Florida more than six hundred skeletons were found. Indians may have died in an epidemic, been killed in war, or suffered from another disaster.

A few mounds were reached by causeways. They were needed to get to mounds built on low swampy land some distance from a village. It was not a common practice to build on low ground.

Not all Indians buried their dead. Some graves were not even marked. Sometimes bodies were placed on frames high out of reach of wild animals. After a time, the bones were buried or placed in burial pots or boxes.

Each camp or village had its shell mound or trash pile which grew larger day by day. The more Indians ate, the higher these mounds became. They were near springs, rivers, salt water, or lakes where a tribe chose to live.

If wild game or sea food were easy to get, the mounds grew faster. They were just great piles of trash made up of anything the people no longer wanted. There were bones of deer, bears, rabbits, or other animals mixed in with empty oyster, clam, scallop, or any shells left from cooking and meals. Broken pottery, broken stone and bone tools, and ashes from cooking fires were there too.

South Florida has many sand and shell mounds that have never been bothered by modern man. They stand in swamps or on off-shore islands where snakes and mosquitoes are thick. Many are deep in the Everglades.

Maybe they were built as platforms where Indians could live above the high water mark of the swamps. Indians dug canals between platforms and others that led to the coast. Sea walls surrounded villages, and causeways connected them. Dugouts, rafts, or skin boats supplied transportation needs.

Generation after generation of Indians chose the same spots to live where fish always seemed to be plentiful and soil always seemed to be good for growing food.

Trash piles of ancient people became many layers deep. Green Mound is so big that a Timucua Indian town may have once been located there. It is between the Halifax River and the Atlantic Ocean. Daytona Beach citizens bought the mound to save it from people who would destroy it.

Our coast and banks of large rivers show that early men knew how and where to pick sites to build large towns. Jacksonville, Miami, St. Augustine, and Tampa were also chosen by intelligent prehistoric Indians as good places to build towns.

Mounds today can easily be mistaken for hills thirty or more feet high. Many were built so long ago that tall trees, vines, thickets, or other kinds of vegetation now cover them.

Chapter 5

➳ There is a right way to study a mound to learn the history of Florida's ancient past. Careless digging mixes everything up so much that valuable history is lost. It's like tearing a page from a book into little pieces and throwing them into the air on a windy day. Nobody can find anything.

Trained researchers mark off a large space into squares several feet wide. They leave walls of earth between these squares. They dig carefully and try to piece together everything they find. What they find is put in museums. This adds more pages to Florida history.

All over Florida searchers have located Indian campsites and villages. They have done this by examining places where canals are being dredged. They have worked where land is being leveled for planting and where ground is being prepared for building houses. They have found scrapers, hammerstones, arrow and spear points, pendants, conch shell beads, flint points, shell tools, and broken pottery.

Pictures were taken from the air of the western shore of Lake Okeechobee near Moore Haven. The pictures showed a big circle with a twenty-foot raised platform in the center. Causeways were built from the platform like spokes in a wheel. Searchers uncovered very old pottery, art works of wood, Spanish gold and silver coins, raw silver and gold, and bones of hundreds of Indians. Some articles found prove that Indians traveled and traded.

A Moore Haven filling station owner found beads, arrowheads, tools, bones, and ornaments. A dragline operator uncovered

a giant sloth with a man-made arrow stuck in it. The sloth lived in Florida many thousands of years ago.

A St. Petersburg builder asked experts from the Florida State Museum to examine a large Indian mound, a burial mound containing a thirteenth-century Indian skeleton. It was very old, perhaps existing before agriculture was known in Florida.

At Pinellas Point three kinds of pottery were found. The oldest kind had palm fibers mixed with clay. A later kind had ground shell mixed with clay. A third kind was not made in Florida, indicating that Indians traveled and traded.

Phillipe Park and Safety Harbor once meant home to many Indians of the Tocobaga tribe. There they built their most important town. Some Colonial artifacts, such as pottery shards, glass, musket balls, and jewelry, were found in the upper levels of the mound.

Maximo Moorings has fossilized animal bones. There are ceremonial, burial, and oyster shell mounds at Crystal River. A mastodon with two pairs of tusks and an elephant-sized ground sloth were uncovered there. Turtle Mound is a shell heap; Osprey has shell and burial; Fort Walton Beach has burial; and Madira Bickel has both burial and ceremonial. Vero Beach, with 2,000 years of continuous occupation, has a ceremonial mound.

Florida citizens are becoming more and more interested in learning about Florida's past history through mounds. Groups of people are organizing Historical Societies all over the state. These people are working with universities to keep records for future generations.

After studying the articles which come from mounds, men know that the earliest-made pottery was poorly constructed. It was made by mixing Spanish moss with clay, then shaping it and putting it in the fire to harden. The moss burned out. This kept the pottery from cracking.

Most of the vessels were used for cooking or storing food. These were left plain buff, gray, or black.

Some pieces were polished, engraved, or painted with designs of red, white, or black.

Bowls, plates, cups, bottles, jars, and pots were made. If a vessel or pot had more than one division, it was often decorated with a human or animal image. Even the poorest Indians made large and well-designed articles.

Early Indians grew tobacco. Men smoked pipes made from pottery or carved from stone. Tools, vessels, mortars and pestles, bowls, spoons, combs, and seats were made of wood. Many articles were made of bone and shell. Woven boxes, mats, shields, and baskets were made of cane. Some were plain, but others were covered with artistic designs.

Pottery-making improved as the years passed. Gradually more and more hunters settled down to live in towns. Two kinds of work that helped to bring about this change were a strong interest in farming and the making of good pottery.

Chapter 6

A tribe is a group of Indians that speak a common language. The group uses the same name, claims the same territory, and has some type of government.

Its culture makes it different from other tribes. That means the way the people of a tribe live. Tools, ceremonies, games, religious meetings, sacrifices, punishments, feasts, and laws all picture a tribe's culture.

Each of the great tribes of Florida had a different culture.

The Calusa Indians lived on the lower west coast. They were strong and ready fighters, always at war.

The Tequesta, fierce but not so warlike, lived on the lower east coast. The Jeaga (Hayaga), a small tribe with three villages, lived at Jupiter Inlet. Their only weapons were knives, but they looked cruel and acted cruel, especially to the English seamen whose ships were wrecked on their shores. They were kinder to the Spanish but seemed to get along better with the French than anyone else. The Ais lived south of Cape Canaveral along the coast and not more than thirty miles inland from the Indian River region.

None of these tribes farmed. Palm berries, coco plums, sea grapes, and fish were used as food. White men found them all hard to get along with and soon learned to keep away from the Calusa, especially.

The Timucua lived in the middle and northeast section. Their language was understood in all parts of the peninsula. When Spanish missionaries came to Florida, they learned Timucuan, then used it to carry on conversations with the Indians wherever they went.

They published textbooks in Timucuan which made it easier to teach different tribes.

Father Pareja, a missionary, lived among the Indians for many years. Some of our earliest valuable records and books about Florida were left by him.

Timucua Indians were active, strong, and tall. One chief was at least half a foot taller than any Frenchman who visited them. Their height, strength, and fine appearance were outstanding when with other tribes. Young and middle-aged Indians fought, ran or swam with ease. Women swam with children on their backs and climbed trees easily.

Good food, exercise, and outdoor living were most important to them. They believed that these things made them strong and active.

They built sturdy homes, cultivated large fields of corn, lived in towns, and were more civilized than tribes of South Florida.

The Apalachee Indians lived west of the Aucilla River in north Florida where they farmed. They were as civilized as the Timucua and were more powerful. Their chiefs worked together in a strong organization.

In recent years San Damian de Escambi Mission was unearthed north of Tallahassee. Near it was an Apalachee Indian cemetery. The mission was set up by the Spaniards and was used for about sixty years. On June 29, 1704, it was destroyed by British soldiers and Creek Indian warriors. In the cemetery were seventy graves.

Searchers thought it must be a Christian cemetery. They found only copper and glass beads in the graves. Priests wouldn't allow anything else to be buried with the dead because that would be a heathen practice.

Mike Skeggs

Chapter 7

The different weather and soil conditions of North and South Florida made it impossible for all tribes to live in the same manner.

South Florida was hot and swampy. In the swamps there were islands or patches of rich soil called hummocks, where hardwood trees grew. There were also tropical jungles. The rest of the land, not suitable for farming, was mostly sand.

Everybody worked to feed the people of a camp. Early Indian women, with the help of the children, gathered berries, seeds, and roots. Men hunted deer, rabbits, and other small animals. When game became scarce, camp was moved – always close to fresh drinking water.

A small band of families made up a camp. A family meant a father, a mother, a daughter, a son or two, and maybe an aunt or uncle. By traveling in small groups of families they made the food supply last longer so it wasn't necessary to move camp so often.

When it was necessary to move, a new camp was made near a shallow bay, near a river, or near salt water. It was always where fish were easy to spear or where oysters, conchs, clams, crabs, scallops, turtles, or alligators were plentiful. To catch fish, ancients set nets made of tough fiber of the Spanish bayonet. They used hooks of shell or bone.

In those days, oysters grew as large as a person's hand. Hard-shell clams often measured six inches across and weighed five pounds or more apiece.

There wasn't any such thing as pottery yet. Fish and meat were eaten raw, dried, roasted over a fire, or cooked in skin bags with water by adding hot stones until the food was tender.

To break camp and move was no problem. Early Indian hunters walked a lot. When moving day came, they collected their fish nets, baskets, skin bags, and scrapers made of shell, deer jaws, or antlers. They took their shell cups, oyster-shell spoons, and shark-tooth knives. They loaded up their spears, spear throwers, stone axes, conch chisels, and shell hammers. They walked out of their palmetto-thatched huts or deerskin tents with their few belongings in bundles. They carried the bundles on their backs or moved them in dugouts to the new camp.

Today, families are often transferred by a company from one section of the country or state to another because of the father's work. The task is made easier if experienced men pack and crate all the furniture. Then a moving van man takes everything to the new home. Sometimes a big transport plane is used to carry the goods. Time has made changes in Florida living.

In North Florida long ago, instead of living in camps, Indians built houses that were the best for them. A house might be round, dome-shaped, rectangular, or square. It might be a one-family palmetto shack or a reed house plastered over with clay. In large towns many families lived in long houses which today we would call apartment houses.

A permanent town had a plaza or square which was divided into two parts. At one end was a mound with the Hot House and Cabin Court built on top of it. In some towns the chief's house was also on the mound. The rest of the plaza was taken up by the chunky yard at ground level. This rectangular yard was banked with earth on three sides. It was used for games, dances, and other amusements.

The Hot House was used as a winter temple and as a men's club. There the chief conducted Council Meetings of tribal leaders. There the shaman, or medicine man, gave new names to successful warriors.

The Hot House was large and round. It was built of posts set on end close together and plastered with mud. The roof was thatched or made of bark. The narrow entrance was protected by overlapping walls.

Around the inside walls were two rows of wide benches built like steps and covered with mats or skins. Nobody had to watch a fire which burned all the time in the center of the room. It was laid in a spiral of dry wood from which bark had been taken to keep it from smoking.

Here warriors could sleep, talk, smoke, loaf, or just listen to music.

The Cabin Court was used in the summer when weather was warm. Four cabins formed the sides of a large square. As in the Hot House, rows of benches were placed around the walls. Each clan had a special place to sit.

Two to a dozen mounds were built around the sides of the square in some towns. People built their homes on the ground all around the mounds. Beyond the homes of the people, gardens and fields extended in all directions.

Sometimes streets and blocks of houses had private garden plots. Family plots were separated by low banks of earth. The men marched together to the field of plots. They carried hoes with stone blades or shoulder blades of animals. Women followed and carried food. All the men and women worked together. An overseer watched as they sang and worked. Any who were lazy were fined. They grew corn, squashes, sweet potatoes, and melons.

Nobody bought land. It belonged to everybody. People "owned" it only while they lived on it.

As do people today, some Indians built two houses, one for summer and one for winter. Carved wooden stools and platforms for beds were almost the only furniture they used. Woven mats of cane or rushes covered the beds.

The home was made up of four separate buildings. An open court was in the center. The winter building was small and warm, with a kitchen. The summer house was open and airy. The third building was used as a storehouse. Part was a shed where tools and equipment were kept. In the fourth building hides and goods for trading were stored.

A high fence of strong log stakes pointed at the top, or of palmetto tree trunks set close together, slanting or straight up, was sometimes built around a village. It kept out wild animals and enemy tribes.

Each gate had a guard house. Often a moat or bank of dirt several feet wide and high surrounded a town. Tribes were almost always at war. The winner carried away the women and children.

Chapter 8

The Indian chief was a leader, not a ruler. Sometimes he was called a king or cacique. A council made decisions. Most always extra food was kept in one storehouse. The chief took as much dried corn, fish, or fruit as he wanted. Anything left was divided among the other Indians or given to war parties. It was also used for feeding visitors, for helping towns that had lost their crops, and for other emergencies.

The chief and leaders of a tribe were chosen from a special clan. They sat on higher stools than other council members. They wore special clothes to show their rank. On important occasions, the chief and council members were carried on litters. Servants held sunshades over them.

For a celebration the chief wore a feather bonnet. He painted his face with certain patterns and colors to show his importance in the community and the town where he lived.

These tribes were sunworshippers. They thought that the chief was descended from the sun itself. They called him the Great Sun. No one had greater authority. His person was sacred, and his foot was not allowed to touch the earth. If he had to walk, mats were spread for him. He was carried everywhere on a litter.

He conducted a ceremony every morning. He howled at the rising sun, then bowed three times. From a sacred pipe he blew smoke to the Four Winds. He made clear to the sun the right path to follow, then went in to eat his breakfast.

The Mound-Building Indians counted temples with sacred fires of first importance. Their religion was closely connected with feasts and celebrations. Many times a year people were brought together in large and small groups.

One ceremony held on a certain day in the spring began at dawn. A stag's head, covered with flowers, was placed on a pole facing east. When first rays of the sun touched the antlered head, the tribe bowed in prayer.

Sometimes small groups celebrated to ask a god for success in hunting, for good weather, or to please an angry god that they feared. If crops were not good, first-born children and captives were sometimes sacrificed during crop planting and harvesting to please the Sun God. The biggest ceremony of all was that held by the farming people.

These Indians worshipped many gods. They respected nature and certain animals. They counted time by the moon and the seasons. The winter moons or months were August, September, October, November, December, and January. Summer moons were February, March, April, May, June, and July.

They believed the earth to be flat. They thought that the sky was a solid cover which was the home of the sky gods. Some tribes had groups of priests to serve the gods.

A priest, storyteller, or healer had to take special training.

A war leader acted as chief of police in times of peace. He also supervised ceremonial games.

MikeSkeggs

Chapter 9

Like most of the races of men, the red Indians sometimes went to war.

Celebrations and ceremonies were held before men went on the war path. Such meetings were frequent, as young men wanted to prove to older people that they had grown up and could take the responsibilities of men.

Older boys were not important in a tribe or group until they convinced the chief that they were strong, skilled, and brave in war and the hunt. If they could do this, they were accepted with respect and were given privileges of men.

A successful young man was given a new name. He had the right to wear certain feathers and could have the story of his victories tattooed on his body.

He used many kinds of weapons, such as stone, reed, or bone knives. He used bows and arrows, darts or spears. For the worst kind of hand-to-hand fighting, warriors used clubs. Sharp pieces of stone or fish teeth stuck out like spikes from these clubs.

When warriors came home, more celebrations and ceremonies took place to honor their victories.

Lacrosse is the only truly American sport. Indians played it more as part of a religious ceremony than as a sport. This was true of several games which were played on a ceremonial ball field.

Indians were taught as children to think fast, shoot straight, and hit the mark. These skills were learned for self protection.

Lacrosse was often played as part of the preparation of going to war. One purpose was to toughen up the braves for hand-to-hand struggles. It was so rough that broken bones were common. Towns or tribes were frequently matched against each other. A team could be made up of from twelve to one hundred warriors on a side.

Players used wooden rackets strung with twisted squirrel skin netting or Indian hemp fiber. Teams tried to carry, throw, bat, or kick a solid wood or a stuffed deerskin ball toward the post. This was a tall pine tree with all the lower branches taken off. If the ball hit the tree, it scored a point. If possible, opponents were kept from doing the same.

Players worked alone or as a team. Each player with or without the ball decided quickly where to go and what to do because an opponent would give him no rest.

Twenty points was a game. Each time a point was made by a team, a stake was set in the ground until there were ten. Then stakes were taken away one at a time until there were none on the winning side.

The losers ran home. Winners marched around the goal and held a stomp dance.

Indians liked to play chunky. One flat, round, smooth, or carved stone about six inches across was needed, together with two poles tapered to flat points at the ends.

Two men ran side by side down the field. One bowled the stone on edge ahead of them. Still running, each man aimed and threw his pole to the place where he thought the stone would stop rolling. The pole that came closest scored. Practice and judgment were needed.

Sometimes Indians ran up and down the field all day playing and betting their possessions on it. They enjoyed games of chance which they played with pebbles or marked sticks.

Women sometimes played games of ball against them.

Indian boys ran races every day. It was good practice to catch food or get away from wild animals or unfriendly Indians.

Sometimes a reed basket was tied to a small tree trunk. Players tried to shoot a ball through the basket.

Indian wars were not as long or as serious as the wars we know today. No tribe wanted to conquer or kill off another tribe. They just wanted scalps or excitement or control of a hunting ground. When winners had what they wanted, the war was over. The losers usually started it up again at a later time.

Young prisoners were adopted.

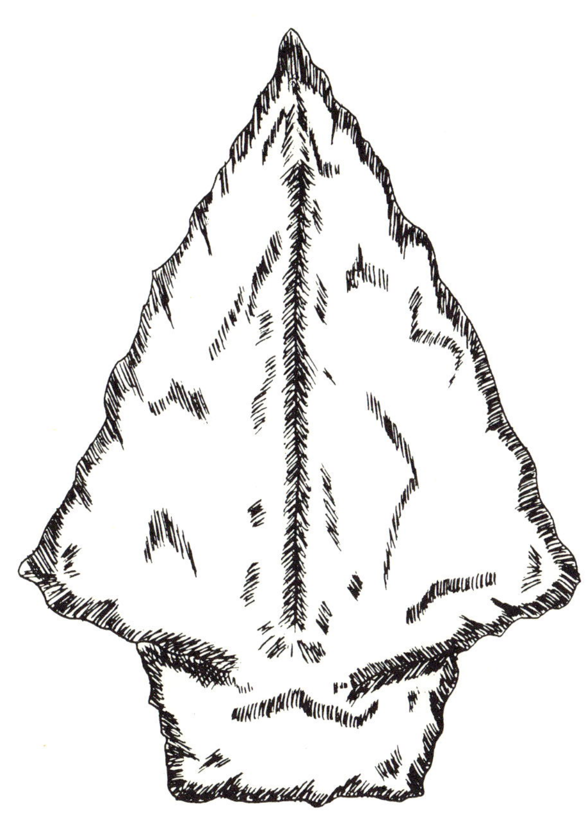

Chapter 10

Indian children were well trained while they were growing up. The mother was mostly responsible for their care, but her brothers helped to train the boys.

Mothers saw to it that girls slept on fawn skins and boys slept on panther skins. They hoped that the children would take in the good qualities of these animals while they slept.

Parents were kind and helpful but strict. If a boy or girl misbehaved, he was scratched on the legs, arms, back, or chest with a sharp-pointed instrument. The jaw of a gar fish was often used. The scratches were deep enough to draw blood. The Indians believed that this let out the evil that caused the trouble and helped the scratched person to be less afraid of losing blood.

A girl always kept the name she was first given, but a boy's name changed many times. If he showed special bravery, courage, or skill, he was given a new one. This showed that he had been promoted in the tribe. It was like moving up one grade higher in school. He never called himself by that name.

Until he corrected his bad traits, a boy was looked down upon by the tribe. He was in disgrace until he proved himself. He had to do all the work nobody else wanted to do even if he were very smart, clever, and intelligent.

When his voice changed, he went off alone to fast for days. This prepared him for danger and responsibility. He had to be strong to survive.

He couldn't take his proper place in the group until he brought in a scalp. That wasn't easy. The first scalp was so important that he sometimes scalped a friend to get it. That didn't mean that the victim would die. If he took home the hair and head skin, he had proof of success. First he surprised his victim, then struck and ran.

To do a good job he struck down the victim. Then he cut a circle in the skin around the crown of the head, raised the edge of the skin at one side and tore it loose with his teeth. He held his trophy by the hair and ran back quickly. He did all this in a few seconds.

Indians learned to stand pain without showing it. They practiced this from childhood. Sometimes two little boys rubbed their heads together until one yielded. Warriors learned to stand such torture that they could talk calmly with their enemies while they were being treated with horrible cruelty.

Chapter 11

Early men who traveled to our continent brought tools made of stone, bone, and shell. Maybe they brought stone knives, bone daggers, and wooden clubs. Harpoons and spear points they made from ivory tusks of mastodons (an ancient type of elephant that once lived in North America). They used spears and spear-throwers to get food and defend themselves from human and animal enemies.

Spear points were stemmed and notched. Notches were either at the sides or bottom of the points. Spear shafts were hollowed out. Spear points were pushed in the hollow parts and tied to the shafts. Weapons like these weighed from two to six pounds.

A spear-thrower was a piece of wood called an atlatl. It was about a foot and a half long with a hook at one end. The bottom of the spear fit into the hook. The hunter held the other end in his hand. He worked fast. He turned his wrist as the spear left the hook. This made it whirl, which gave speed and force to the action necessary to conquer an opponent.

Such weapons helped early Indians overpower huge beasts. The animals were driven into swamps. When the giant bison, thick-skinned mastodons, saber-tooth cats, or other prey became bogged-down and powerless to escape, the pursuers closed in and killed them at close range. On large hunting parties, a herd was first surrounded by fire. Hunters made sure that the wind blew from the game toward them.

The same trick was used in deer hunting. When two teams worked together, one team acted as herders. They chased the deer toward the second team, hiding and waiting with raised spears near a pond, swamp, or man-built trap. The herders made loud noises, beat brush, or set a line of grass fire to help drive the animals toward the second team.

Alligator hunters also worked in teams. Men worked fast as there was great danger. Hunters picked out the alligator they wanted then pushed a long pointed pole down its throat. They turned it over and attacked the softer underbelly ^ with clubs. Hundreds of years later somebody brought bows and arrows across the Bering Strait land bridge to our continent. Several hundred years passed before these weapons finally reached Florida. Then bows and arrows gradually replaced spear-throwers.

A hunter often worked alone. If he wanted to kill a deer, he made plans a long time before he was ready to hunt.

First he carefully removed the head, antlers, and skin from a deer that had been killed. He let this get completely dry. Some time later, when he was ready to go hunting, he covered himself with this disguise. It was a very good one. He could get quite close to a deer without frightening it.

Men fished with spears, bows and arrows, traps, nets, or with hooks and lines.

Arrow-heads were made of flint, horn, or bone by the men who used them.

Muskogee (Creek and Apalachee) Indians carried a quiver and bow case made of panther skin with the fur left on the outside. A fine hickory bow was put into it. Since cane is lightweight, brittle, and straight, it was used for arrows, along with wood, to make them fly straight.

A few Indians used slings and cane knives. Birds and small animals were killed with blowguns.

Before a hunt an Indian performed a special ceremony. He took a sweat bath in a little hut. As he poured water over hot stones, brought to him by someone outside, he prayed and sang. Then he cooled off by diving into the creek. He drank "magic" medicine and put some on his weapons.

Each time he made a campfire on the trail, he burned tobacco leaves to keep evil away. He scratched his own thigh and bled a little to make him strong again. A medicine man went with him to work magic when it was needed. His pay was one deerskin.

Successful hunters and fishermen were generous. They gave some meat or fish to their parents and some to the widows and orphans of the town.

In a year, six hunters could supply a whole camp with clothing. Deerskin was tanned to make it dry, then wetted to make it soft. It wore better than cloth because it was stronger and lasted longer. It was the best available material, not only for clothing but also for moccasins and thongs.

Stiff tail hair was used for ornaments and embroidery. Antlers made good tool handles and arrow points. Hoofs furnished glue and rattles. Claws were used for jingles on belts and anklets as well as for rattles. Sinews provided thread, bowstrings, and snares. Bones were used for bodkins, skin-dressing tools, handles, and ornaments. Bladders and pouches were used as bags and all kinds of containers.

The meat was food for the hungry Indian. Life would have been very difficult without deer.

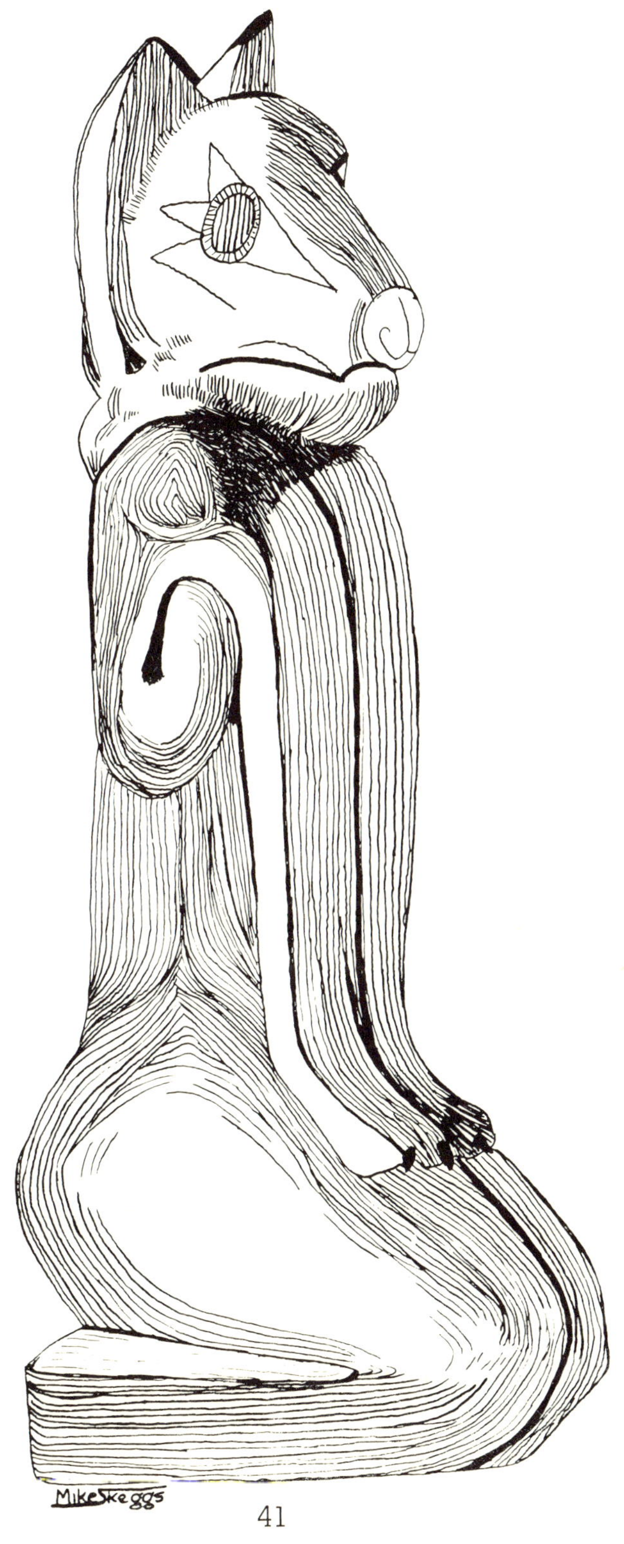
MikeSkeggs

Chapter 12

Indian cultures are mixed up because these people traveled and traded all the time.

The more powerful tribes located their villages along the seashore, at the mouth or banks of a great river, or where two rivers joined. This made it easier to travel and carry on trade.

North Florida Indians, who lived in towns and farmed where soil was good away from the coast, didn't travel much to the sea. Coast Indians often visited them. They took along smoked fish and shell articles to use in trade.

Today we travel and trade too. Oranges, grapefruit, strawberries, fresh vegetables and flowers are shipped north. In exchange we receive apples, tools, and many other products that Florida doesn't have. At the grocery, florist, hardware store, airport, furniture store, and hundreds of other places we trade money for services and merchandise.

Indians traveled by foot, raft, and cypress dugout.

They marked many land trails. Rivers were trails for the dugouts which were left at river crossings.

Cypress dugouts were strong, light, and not easily damaged by water.

To make a dugout, a log was hollowed and shaped by fire. Stone tools such as axes and chisels were used for finishing. Shells made good scrapers. The outside was shaped first. The bottom was about one and one half inches thick when finished. A fire was built on sand in the bottom of the dugout if the weather were cold.

A dugout was light enough to paddle or pole in shallow water.

Some Indian traders traveled as far away as North Carolina, Georgia, Alabama, and Ohio. They sold or traded fine arrowheads, cups made of shell, dippers, hairpins, and necklaces. In exchange they received buckskin, arrow cases, and red paint.

North Carolina Indians exchanged mica, to be made into jewelry, for sea shells and dried fish brought by Florida traders. Mica is transparent. It differs in appearance from colorless to pale yellow or brown to green or black. Once thin sheets of colorless mica were used in lanterns and doors of stoves. It was called isinglass. Some is transparent, sparkling and silvery in appearance. It made attractive ornaments.

Georgia and Alabama Indians made stone axes and chisels to trade for Florida products.

Ohio Indians liked the carved alligator teeth and shell articles from Florida. For these they exchanged thick pieces of copper, which were carried back by the travelers to make into pins, bracelets, and beads.

Long distance travelers and traders made trips as far away as Lake Superior. They returned to Florida by way of Mexico and Cuba with polished stone and copper. Florida Indians fashioned these materials into pottery, pendants, and objects for ceremonies.

Many old Indian trade routes across the country are now four-lane highways.

Tampa Bay Indians didn't venture far from home. They traded, mostly with each other, such products as fish, shells, and pottery.

When Spanish explorers and soldiers came to Florida to get rich and become famous, Indians traded with them. The Spanish were quick to learn that Indians would trade valuable furs and food for cheap articles like mirrors, glass beads, and silver pendants.

An Indian pocket-book must have been clumsy to carry when

conch shells and hair tubes were used as money. For trading away from the coast, one tube was worth four deerskins.

Counting was done with sticks. An Indian who had to go to a meeting in six days put six sticks in a bundle. He threw away one every day until all were gone. It was then time to go.

An arm length, a knuckle length, or a hand width served as an Indian ruler for measuring short lengths. If a trip were long, distance from here to there was measured by so many "sleeps."

Indian mounds and museums give proof that early Florida inhabitants were pretty good treasure hunters. The Bahama Channel is south of Cape Canaveral. The narrowest part is a thirty-nine-mile-wide strip of rough and dangerous water. Ponce de Leon discovered it. Spanish treasure ships used it to sail from Cuba to Spain because it speeded up their slow-moving vessels.

Currents were swift, rocks were hidden, and ships were wrecked. Florida Indians watched for these helpless ships and took all kinds of treasure from them.

We are treasure hunters too. Today we take treasure from Indian mounds and put it in museums. We are keeping Florida history.

Stone Age men conquered distance from far-away lands on foot, by raft, or by skin boat. Today's travelers reach Florida in air-conditioned ships, trains, airplanes, or automobiles. Their food is provided. They need not hunt mammoths and mastodons to get it, as Stone Age travelers did.

Chapter 13

Very early Florida Indians didn't worry too much about clothes. As the weather was mild, their clothes served more as ornaments.

Men wore breach clouts made of braided palm fiber and went barefoot around home. Warriors wore moccasins for travel or ceremonies. Another mark of a warrior was a snakeskin belt from which hung a fringe of shredded bark. When he dressed up, he wore a robe covered with bird feathers. He wore a pouch slung from one shoulder. This was for his pipe, tobacco, a magic stone, and powdered red paint. When weather became colder, an animal skin served as a robe, and buckskin leggings covered his legs.

Women wore short skirts of Spanish moss or deerskin and one or two necklaces. In colder weather they wore longer skirts or woven bark tunics hung over one shoulder. Tunics were as soft as cloth.

For celebrations, important Indians wore feather bonnets and hung gorgets or carved shell disks around their necks. Rulers and priests of high rank wore costumes of bright colors made with great care. Some were feather cloaks made by fastening feathers to netting. Some robes were made of muskrat skins.

Fingernails and toenails were kept long. Both men and women painted their skins and tattooed their bodies. When Indians were very important, tattooing was carefully designed.

Ornaments were made of copper, stone, bone, shell, wood, clay, feathers, and pearls. They were worn on the neck, arms, and legs. Some of these were rattles, armbands, legbands, pendants, necklaces, beads, rings, ear ornaments, and hairpins. Gorgets or metal breastplates of copper or carved shell were worn as neck ornaments or armor to protect the throat. An Indian brave pierced his ears and wore in them blown up fish bladders dyed red. Some Indians wore wooden ear buttons that looked like big cuff buttons two inches in diameter.

Hair styles changed from tribe to tribe. A Timucuan Indian piled his long hair high in a knot on top of his head. The knot was a good place to keep extra arrows.

Bone or polished tortoise shell hairpins helped keep hair in place.

Some Indians cut one side close and left the other side long. Some shaved the top and left a fringe around the edge. Creek men shaved their heads but left a crest from front to back.

Sometimes hair was plucked. A piece of obsidian or flint was split to a thin strip so sharp that it could be used as a razor.

Heron feathers were used for turban or hair decorations. If ostrich plumes were used, they were secured in trade.

As they traveled, the Indians learned new hair styles from various tribes and adopted them.

Everybody soaked hair in bear grease.

Some women let their long hair fall loose. Others wore it in a roll or braids. In a few tribes it was bound up after a woman married. When a husband died, his widow cut her hair short and couldn't marry anybody else until it covered her shoulders again.

Mike Skeggs
86

Chapter 14

M Indians were quiet, calm, and silent. They were trained to be that way. When others talked, they listened. When it was their turn, they understood what to say and how to say it. White people were impressed with their good manners, good posture, and dignity.

When we meet our friends, we sometimes shake hands, but Indian friends held arms. To promise friendship they scratched each other with the toothed jawbone of a gar fish.

Before a lacrosse game players were scratched. When they were promoted, warriors were scratched.

A sign language was commonly used.

Whoops meant different things to friends. One kind was for telling news, one for showing anger, one for announcing a death, and another for taking a scalp.

When Indians went visiting, they sat quietly for a short time and said nothing. That was their way for being polite. Later they talked and made speeches. If an Indian came home from a trip, he told the whole story with all the details.

Everybody tried not to hurt the feelings of another person.

A visiting stranger was entertained by the town. He was fed from the chief's storehouse and he slept in the special house for guests.

Indians knew what to do on the trails and in the forest. They understood nature, the ways of birds, animals, winds, and storms. They taught the white men where to catch fish, how to cultivate tobacco, and how to raise corn, beans, and squashes. They taught them wood craft and games such as lacrosse. Medicine men taught them how to use plants as cures when people were sick.

The forest people didn't understand the bad manners of white men. Selfishness and refusal to share food and clothing, even when they had more than they needed, showed rudeness.

Indians were respectful. White men could practice their own religion and Indians didn't make fun of it. They could go to the white man's church and be honest in their worship, then go to their own service and believe it too. There was good in both.

If a couple decided to get married, the man broke an ear of corn in two. He gave half to the bride together with the foot of a deer. He left deer meat at her door. She cooked the meat and fed some to him before witnesses. The couple always lived in the wife's village.

When Spanish missionaries worked with the tribes of North Florida, the Timucua and Apalachee, many Indians became Christians. White priests lived near their villages and taught them to live civilized lives.

In the 1700's Creeks from Georgia took the side of the English against the Spaniards who then claimed Florida. They made raids all the way to the Everglades and captured thousands of cattle. Their owners were sold as slaves in New England and the West Indies.

Two hundred years after white men came to Florida, the old tribes were gone.

Chapter 15

Mounds were built by early Indian tribes in Florida years and years before Christopher Columbus landed on the island of San Salvador. When white explorers sailed to the coast of Florida in strange winged ships, the curious Mound Building Indians gazed in wonder. They were courteous and welcomed the strangers as friends and guests.

They brought to the explorers expensive gifts. They wanted to share advice, food, land, and freedom. They felt that the land belonged to all and no man had a right to claim any for himself. The sun, earth, plants, and animals made life possible. They were thankful and worshipped them.

Indians watched the ways of wild animals, admired their skill, and wished they could talk to them. Forest trees seemed almost to be people. Storm clouds, thunder, tornadoes, hurricanes, and unusual weather made the red men feel helpless before a mighty unseen power. They were very sincere.

White men the Indians met weren't like that. They soon learned how easy it was to get what they wanted from the Indians. They took all they could get and even forced the Indians to keep on giving.

The Indians tried to be kind by giving more and more to the explorers and settlers. The white men could never be satisfied.

Columbus was sure that he had reached India. He called the people Indians. When he returned to Spain, he took warriors back with him to show to the people of Europe.

He didn't know that the ancestors of these warriors were Stone Age men. He didn't know that they had been mound builders for years and were still building mounds. He also didn't know that North and South America, like a vast wall, blocked his path to India.

Ponce de Leon and other explorers landed on the Florida mainland, but thought they were on an island. They called the people Indians because Columbus did.

The Spanish king had no idea how far Nova Scotia was from Florida. He didn't know that all the land between was filled with tribes that spoke as many as 200 languages. He declared it all a part of Florida.

Explorers and settlers kept coming to Florida. After a long, long time, Indians began to realize how greedy these new people were. They became less generous.

White men killed their people, burned their villages, and took their land. Finally, the Indians began to treat their guests as they had been treated. It took so long because they still believed that everybody shared alike in the good things of the earth. Nobody owned anything himself.

An Indian killed to get food but did not make it a habit to torture helpless animals or people. That happened after he learned through experience to defend himself from cruel white men. His life in the forest had not prepared him to expect such treatment.

Tribes were well organized for the time in which these people lived. Many cultures were of a very high order. Indians were sincere in their religious beliefs and had their own high standards of living.

Explorers didn't always realize that they were dealing with intelligent people who knew right from wrong and lived in an orderly manner. Tribes naturally resented cruelty of land-hungry, gold-hungry strangers. Indians had lived on the land for thousands of years before explorers and settlers arrived. They fought to keep their homes.

Guns, gunpowder, well-trained dogs, and a few soldiers could conquer hundreds of Indians who had only crude weapons, bows and arrows, and their own cleverness to depend on to help them. Much of their skill was learned from watching wild animals.

From the start they had no chance against greedy white people. They worked – not for wealth – only to feed themselves. They were disorganized helpless victims of white people who took their land, destroyed their Indian societies, institutions and cultures, but not their respect for nature.

An Indian long ago explained to his people the meaning of life. He said, "It is the flash of a firefly in the night. It is the little shadow which runs across the grass and loses itself in the sunset."

The Indians understood.

Chapter 16

The Seminoles are Florida's newest Indians. Two hundred and seventy-five years ago there was no such thing as a Seminole Indian.

The Apalachee, the Timucua, the Tocobaga, the Ais, the Jeaga, the Tequesta, the Calusa, and many more lived in Florida when Spain owned it. Many were killed or carried off in raids of white settlers, many died in epidemics, and others left Florida with the Spaniards when England took it in 1763. Florida just didn't have any aboriginal Indians left.

In 1750 the Seminoles moved in and occupied the land where once the Mound Building Indians lived.

Between the Apalachicola River and the St. Johns River in north Florida was a large area of land. Some Creek tribes from Georgia and Alabama used it as a hunting ground.

A number of small tribes joined the big Creek Indian group, which became very strong. Part of the Creek nation became friends of the English traders who offered them better-made goods than the Spaniards did. They liked the advantages of living close to white people, so they stayed where they were.

The Oconee Indians, another part of the large Creek group, did not like the English. They wanted to live as their fathers and grandfathers had. They wanted freedom to swim, fish, gather wild honey, and hunt deer and bear.

They knew about the hunting grounds in north middle Florida and went there to live. They also knew that they could do as they pleased and nobody would bother them. They became known as the Seminoles, a Creek word meaning "Wild People." They broke away from the "tame" Indians who remained near the English.

Although Spain claimed all of Florida, the king was mainly interested in the east coast. He had to protect his treasure-filled ships that sailed through the Florida Straits and the Bahama Channel. Other countries that sent soldiers and ships to take Florida away from Spain didn't worry him. Florida was too far away from the Old World for them to succeed. His big troubles were right at home where other countries were fighting wars with Spain.

Middle Florida was a long way from any Spanish towns. The Seminoles kept to themselves except to do a little trading with friendly Spaniards.

These Indians made their own laws and settled their own troubles. Seacoffee, or Cow-keeper, was their chief. Some owned farms, orange groves, Negro slaves, and cattle. The slaves had run away from white owners. Some slaves left other tribes and joined the Seminoles.

The Negro slaves lived in towns by themselves. They were given tools and were made to pay rent. They built palmetto houses with palmetto roofs. They kept cattle and horses. They planted corn, potatoes, rice, and beans. They gave food to their Indian masters.

In return the Seminoles gave to the slaves safety from other tribes and from white people. When there was a war, both Seminoles and Negroes worked together to guard their homes. The Negroes were happy and the Seminoles were happy.

All went well until 1821, when the United States took over the territory of Florida from Spain. The Spanish governor at St. Augustine always let the Seminoles use any land that they wanted. The United States, the new owner, did not do this.

Americans wanted the rich farm land where the Seminoles lived. The Seminoles knew this and tried desperately to save their homes. Although they fought bravely, their fields were taken, their homes were burned, and their cattle were destroyed.

Many Indians were killed or sent out of the territory. Americans kept pushing them farther south and kept working to get them to go to Oklahoma territory to live. Some Indians felt they had a right to live in Florida and refused to leave. Three wars were fought before the United States finally stopped the fighting to save money and lives.

Seminole and Negro warriors altogether didn't number more than 1200. The United States had thousands of trained men. Over three thousand lost their lives. Indians knew the trails, swamps, and best places to make surprise attacks. They had the advantage because they fought on home territory.

This is a story about the Seminole War. It was told to little Yeh-cah-yee by her grandmother. Yeh-cah-yee is now a very old woman, more than eighty years old.

"My grandmother little girl then. Indians live in many camps. Always on move from camp to camp. Soldiers hunt Indians. Indian men fight soldiers until women and children get away. Many Indian men die from soldiers' guns. Many women and children caught by soldiers, carried away from home to other lands.

"People live on animals and birds and fish they catch. They plant corn and beans in hidden fields. But soldiers come, burn camps, hunt for fields to destroy crops. Drive Indian back and back until Indian surrounded in big swamp. Not many Indians left. Others killed or caught. Indians hide on islands in big swamp. In time white man no come to hunt Indian. No more fighting. War over."

For many years Yeh-cah-yee's people lived in fear of white men and she cannot forget their mistrust. Even today she is unhappy around white men.

She was named by her grandmother who fought in the Seminole War. Her name, Yeh-cah-yee, comes from the song of the medicine men.

Girls are sometimes given the names of creatures, such as birds or frogs.

Today Indian girls go to school to learn English. When Yeh-cah-yee was little, she was not permitted to learn English or even to talk to white people.

Her mother and grandmother slept in chickees. She will do the same as long as she lives. Children growing up today will never do that.

In another ten years it is thought that a chickee will be nothing more than a memory, although it seems well adapted to the climate of the Everglades.

Chapter 17

A shaman or medicine man was highly respected. He spent his time in curing sick people, practicing magic, controlling the weather, and telling what will happen in the future.

Many Indians today trust medicine men instead of modern science. The medicine men depend on several herb teas and special songs to help the spirits in healing the sick.

Today there is only one medicine man in the Big Cypress. He is Josie Billie, now over eighty years old. He has served the Seminole tribe as a medicine man all his life.

He lived very close to nature in a cypress hammock. From the time he was young, he seemed to understand the secret powers of herbs and roots. For twenty years he studied and learned more before he really began to help his people in sickness. Older men in the tribe saw that he learned quickly about Indian medicine. They chose him for this work.

Josie Billie waits for patients to come to him. He helps only when asked. He also waits for someone to teach to be a medicine man. He can't ask others. They must ask him. Children today go to school to learn to read and write, not to learn medicine.

He is so good that once he went to Michigan to tell some doctors about herbs for sickness. Some Indians pay him in moccasins, material, a chicken, or a deerskin. He is not permitted to ask for money for some sicknesses.

He says, "Good thing about white doctor's medicine, it keeps. Indian medicine, no keep."

Today most Indians are treated at the free clinic on the reservation. A white doctor, sent by the division of Indian Health under the United States Public Health Service, takes care of them.

Chapter 18

Men are often named for Indian war heroes. Osceola is a favorite name used today.

The famous Osceola was a war leader. He did more for his people than many a Seminole chief ever thought of doing.

Osceola wore three ostrich feathers in his head band. Most chiefs wore heron feathers. He wore one white plume and two black plumes in the back. He never seemed to do things the way most people did. Even when he was a little boy playing with the other children, he was different.

After a hard day of play if mothers asked their children, "Who was the best ball player today?" the answer was always, "Osceola." "Who was your leader?" "Osceola."

Energy and determination kept him first.

Years passed. Mothers asked "Who is our Seminole war leader?" They always hoped that one of their sons might win the honor of being first, but the answer was still "Osceola."

About fifty years before Osceola was born, the first group of Seminoles left the Creek Nation and traveled to Florida, then owned by Spain. Fifty years later a second group left the Creeks and joined the Seminoles. Osceola's mother and her young son came to Florida with this group.

Even when he was little, he was very independent. He did many things for himself, was quick to see what was going on about him, decided what he wanted, then quietly worked to get it. He grew up while Spain was losing Florida for the last time, and the United States was gaining it as a territory.

He saw the changes from Spanish rule to American rule. As more and more white men came to make homes in the territory, he watched his people struggle to hold their own lands.

He watched settlers take land from his people, drive off their cattle, and burn their homes. He saw Seminoles fight back by doing the same to the settlers. He was fiercely loyal to the Seminoles and believed that Florida was theirs.

He began to attend Council meetings and listened to the chiefs. They were the only people who were permitted to speak. Osceola knew he had no right to speak but saw that Chief Micanopy was not trying to help the tribe as much as he should.

Osceola sat by him and told him what to say. At first the other chiefs didn't like this. After a while they saw that he had good judgment, ability, and intelligence. They made him their war leader.

He was always polite, always a gentleman, always treated white men with dignity, and always spoke in the Indian language. He was a good speaker. People listened and followed his advice. He spoke his thoughts freely, and whether others liked it or not, always gave his honest opinion.

He sent a message to General Clinch during the Second Seminole War. "You have guns, so have we. You have powder and lead, and so have we. Your men will fight, and so will ours 'til the last drop of Seminole blood has moistened the dust of his hunting ground."

General Thompson asked the chiefs to sign papers to leave Florida at once and go west of the Mississippi River to live. He threatened them if they refused. Osceola was so angry that he jumped up, pinned the paper to the desk with his dagger and cried, "The only treaty I will execute is with this!"

The Seminoles asked to stay in Florida. The government made

plans to ship them west. If they moved west of the Mississippi, they would have no lightwood. They would have to live again with the Creeks, the tribe from which they had once run away.

Impatient young braves wanted war. Osceola master-minded the plans. Some chiefs planned to move west, but Osceola and his band either killed them or drove them away. He asked all the Seminoles to stay in Florida. All the chiefs who were left joined his band.

Although he didn't like white people, he liked children. He always advised his warriors to act like men. There was to be no war with women and children. The scalping knife was to be saved for men. His warriors sometimes forgot.

Osceola went to see General Thompson on business. He was thrown in chains, but later freed. He never forgot or forgave the general. Later Osceola killed the general and planned the death of Major Dade and his men. These two events started the Seminole War between the United States and the Seminoles.

After hopeless fighting, Osceola and some of his men asked to meet with white men near St. Augustine. When the Indians arrived, they were arrested and sent to prison. Wild Cat or Coacoochee escaped. Nineteen others escaped with him through a little window high in the prison wall.

Osceola was sick and could not go with his men. The next day he told General Jessup what had happened. Osceola and the other prisoners were sent to Ft. Moultrie, a very strong prison, at Charleston, South Carolina. About a month later Osceola died there.

When someone painted his picture, Osceola always put on his complete war dress. He was very proud.

He insisted that his family help him to put on his full war dress and war paint when he knew that he would die but was too weak to do much for himself.

Counties, towns, lakes, streets, and avenues have been named after him. Many books have been written about him.

Osceola would have been greatly surprised if he could have attended funeral services for his grandson, William McKinley Osceola. Three great-grandsons of the famous warrior, Osceola, and three white men carried the coffin. The chief, William Osceola, was buried in a scarlet medicine jacket and handstitched leggings. The service was read both in English and in Seminole. He was buried in a white man's cemetery.

William, grandson of the great war leader, Osceola, learned English and sent his sons to public schools in Miami. He died while watching a Green Corn Dance ceremony deep in the Everglades.

Every day, Seminoles and white men learn to get along together better. Many great changes have taken place in less than 150 years' time.

Chapter 19

After Wild Cat, or Coacoochee, escaped through the little window high up in the prison wall of Fort Marion, or Castillo de San Marcos, he took Osceola's place. He encouraged the Seminole chiefs to fight. He took part in almost every important attack himself.

Once near St. Augustine he attacked a group of actors and took their costumes. These were worn when they acted out plays by William Shakespeare. Not long after that he went to a council meeting all dressed up in stage clothes. He must have looked as strange to those at the meeting as an astronaut would today if he attended church in his space suit.

He lived up to his name, Wild Cat. He was a small man as swift and active as a deer.

He was the most dangerous of the Seminole chiefs. War excited him and made him happy. It kept him busy. He and his band raced up and down the St. Johns River, filling everybody with terror by burning, killing, and destroying. When soldiers chased him through deep swamps, he watched them from a distance as they stumbled and floundered through mud and water with their weapons. He laughed and made fun of them.

He was very clever and kept the fighting going for seven years. Then he and his band went west of the Mississippi River too. Sam Jones and Billy Bowlegs were the only chiefs left.

Chief Boleck was known to everybody as Billy Bowlegs. He could write his name, something only a few Indians could do. Most Indians signed papers with an "X."

Billy knew how to use tools and fix machines.

One time he stopped at a trading post near the Everglades. The storekeeper had a broken music box. It was supposed to play five tunes, but it played only a few notes. Billy had some things that he wanted to trade. The storekeeper asked Billy to trade what he had for the music box. He told Billy, "music no more play – wake up by and by and play good – him tired now." Billy made the trade and left with the "tired" music box under his arm.

The next day Billy was back with the music box. He showed the box to the trader and said, "That box, him no more tired. Him play good at Green Corn Dance down Okeechobee."

He wound up the machine. It played all five tunes.

Billy Bowlegs started the Third Seminole War because white men tore up his garden and banana patch for fun, and he showed them he wouldn't stand for that. The war lasted two years.

The government offered him a large sum of money to go west. He finally accepted a larger sum and with his followers moved to Oklahoma.

John Jumper was a chief sent to Indian Territory, or Oklahoma, as it is called today. He fought with white men in the Civil War and became Colonel John Jumper.

He was music leader of his tribe. A missionary taught him a song of the white men. He changed it into the Seminole language. Florida Seminoles know the song. They learned it from Indians living on a reservation in Oklahoma.

Chapter 20

The Spaniards brought to Florida from Spain both sweet and sour oranges. They planted trees. Indians liked the fruit. As they traveled, they ate the oranges and threw away seeds. After a time the seeds grew into wild orange trees. Some wild trees still grow in Florida. Both trees and fruit are beautiful to see but the oranges are very sour and bitter.

Tiger Tail was a Seminole who seemed to get along well with white people. On Sunday he always wore clean and respectable clothing. He was friendly and spent his time in fishing or hunting, then selling or trading with white settlers.

He was tall and well built. A red calico shirt, fringe of yellow beads, feathered head dress, leggings, and moccasins was an outfit he once wore. He crossed the garden with a quick, direct walk and threw a wild turkey and a bunch of quail at the feet of a prospective customer. Without another greeting he muttered, "Fifty cents."

Wild oranges grew near his camp on the east coast. He took a load of these oranges to a small town. A train stopped at the town. When people on the train saw the fruit, they wanted to buy. Tiger Tail asked one cent for each orange.

People wanted to pay more. They gave him twenty-five cents a dozen. They knew the price of sweet oranges and wanted to be fair. Those who first tasted the fruit kept quiet until all of the oranges were sold. Then they asked everybody to taste the oranges. The people laughed and threw sour oranges at Tiger Tail as the train pulled away.

Tiger Tail couldn't understand why everybody threw oranges

at him. He counted his money. He had twenty-five dollars. This was much more than he expected to get. Then he knew what had happened. The white men thought his oranges were sweet. They paid him the price of sweet oranges. He had been honest and the white men had been honest.

Afterward Tiger Tail gave this explanation: "White man no like Tiger Tail's oranges – sour too much. Me tell white man one orange, one cent. White man tell me one orange, two cents. Indian no cheat white man."

Tiger Tail had no thought of cheating, but it looked that way. Indians learn not to cheat when they are children.

Chapter 21

A The Seminole may be changing many of his ways to suit the world of the white man, but he still keeps the customs and laws of his ancestors. This is hard for many white people to understand.

Indians have their own way of determining values. Something that would mean a lot to a white person might have no worth for an Indian.

White men work very hard for money, comfort, and power. Indians believe in working with nature, not controlling it. In days past, Indians worked together, not against each other. There were no jails, no police, and no crime.

All worked for the good of the community, not self. Today most Indians don't belong in a city. Factory and office work are not for them. Outdoor living on well-developed reservations, surviving as a separate race and learning tribal traditions about the family campfire are better for them.

Education in the white men's schools and working together will bring about better understanding between white men and Indians.

A few years ago Seminole children were discouraged from learning the white men's ways. Today they are beginning to do the same kind of work, go to the same schools, see the same TV programs, and drive on the same highways.

Indians want comforts, security, and law protection that white men have, but want to be a race of people apart.

Indians feel obligated. They won't take loans unless they can meet payments. They respect the rights of other people.

The title of Chief is not passed from father to son. It is passed from the Chief to his sister's son.

In the past Indians wrote no books. They don't talk much and their history is not too reliable. They are not banded together as a group with one powerful central leader. An Indian often changed his name over the years, and spelling wasn't always the same. A name was spelled as it sounded to the listener. Seminoles do not speak easily to strangers. This has helped them to keep many of their ancient tribal customs.

Their religion includes an all-powerful God who made laws of good behavior for his people. Breaking God's law is more serious than violating the laws made by man. Being honest and honorable come first.

A man lives with his wife's family. Children take the mother's name instead of the father's. A woman owns the house, furnishings, chickens, pigs, and all clothing except that worn by the husband. She also rears the children. The husband owns all fishing and hunting equipment, horses, and cows, except milk cows.

The mother's brother or nearest living relative disciplines children. The clan is passed down through women. A clan is usually named after an animal. Some clan names are Bear, Fox, Wildcat, Skunk, Buzzard, Alligator, Otter and Water Moccasin. The clans do not intermarry.

A most important custom carried over from ancient times is the Green Corn Dance. Great numbers of people meet deep in the Everglades. White men are not invited, as this is the time to settle all tribal matters. Any business which concerns the good of the tribe is discussed. Family and business disputes are settled. A medicine man conducts the meeting. A tribal council of chiefs passes judgment and makes all decisions. Almost a week is needed to complete the whole program.

An Indian who has broken a law or custom of the tribe is punished. If he is ever punished at a Green Corn Dance, he won't forget it. To cheat, to lie, or to steal are great wrongs.

If he is found guilty of murder, he is banished from the group. No Seminole will ever speak to him again. If he is condemned to die, the clan that suffered the loss carries out the penalty. If death was an accident, the guilty Indian must support the wife and children of the dead man.

The spring gathering of older tribes celebrated the beginning of a new year. A real housecleaning took place. Old clothes were burned. Old cooking utensils were broken or thrown away. All the fires in town were put out, even the fire in the Hot House. Embers from the temple fire were used to start a new one. Wood for a new fire was laid in the Cabin Court. Four sticks pointed to the four winds. Four ears of green corn were laid across the sticks. The ends touched and they formed a square. Prayers and magic followed. The chief started a new sacred fire from which all town fires were relighted.

Warriors stopped fasting and ate the first green corn cooked over the new fire. During the Green Corn Dance, the "Black Drink," a strong black tea made from an ancient recipe, was taken by the men. They drank it hot from large gourds to cleanse both body and soul.

After all business was finished and all bad Indians were properly punished, the rest of the week was taken up by ceremonies. There were ritual dances, social dances, games, songs, and feasts.

Seminoles who have not joined Christian churches still go to the Green Corn Dances.

A great gathering in the fall of the year was held to thank the Great Spirit for a good harvest. This took place after the corn was gathered and stored.

Indians dance many dances for many purposes. The ritual of an Indian dance is accompanied by great ceremony. Each dance has a fixed pattern which must be strictly followed. This requires long training. A dancer acts out a play. For example, he tracks an enemy and conquers him. His costume is of the best with no feather out of place. He must have skill and grace. Important parts of the ritual are sung.

An Indian is obligated to his community. He must help others by giving food, shelter, money, or materials to anyone who needs them. Even if a person is not liked, he will still be helped in any way necessary.

Almost always, coming to live permanently with a tribe is open to all.

Chapter 22

Until 1930, Seminole women wore blouses and full-length skirts. For ceremonies they added a cape. Men wore long shirts that look very much like a woman's dress. All clothes had designs. Boot-type moccasins and leggings were made of soft cream-colored doeskin.

Seminole women and girls who live along the Tamiami Trail wear long skirts to hide their bare feet. These full skirts are made of many small bright colored pieces put together to make unusual designs. Blouses with long sleeves are slipped over their heads. They fall loosely from shoulders to hips.

This style was started about seventy years ago. Almost every home has a hand-turned sewing machine, if nothing else. Women sit on the floor to sew.

Some Seminole women wear so many strings of beads that their necks are covered up to their chins. In the past, each Seminole girl received a gift of colored glass beads. Each birthday or special occasion after that she was given another necklace. By the time she was a grandmother she was carrying around twenty-five or thirty pounds of glass beads. As she grew older, the strands were taken off one at a time until the last strand was reached. She wore this until she died.

The old custom is changing. Today most women wear a few strings of beads or no beads at all.

Indian women sometimes wear leggings to dance. These are covered with hundreds of bells made from little hoofs of deer. The bells help to keep time to the music. Other dancers strap to their ankles small dried turtle shells filled with pebbles for the same reason.

Today most Indian girls and young women wear their hair short and get permanent waves. Once all Seminole women let their hair grow very long. They tried different styles but finally settled on one that is as famous as the clothes they make out of such little pieces of bright cloth.

This style has been unchanged for almost seventy years. Hair is combed from the back, forward over a frame of cardboard, wire, or palmetto. This frame helps to hold the hair high. Hairpins and a net keep all in place.

At first you think that these women wear hats, but they don't. This hat-shaped hair-do is now the Seminole trademark. Anything sold at an Indian camp or tourist shop with such a trademark means that it was made by Seminole Indians. Palmetto dolls are always dressed this way.

Most Indian men are changing styles too. Some do not care to change. They are the older Seminoles who wear tunics made of little pieces of cloth worked into a brightly-colored pattern. The pattern tells how important the man who wears it is in the family.

A belt or bright red sash is worn with the tunic and falls to the knees. Close-fitting deerskin leggings, with fringed seams and cuffs, and a high turban fastened with a pointed bone or a fancy pin complete the costume.

Young men buy bright scarves and blue jeans or trousers in the city stores to wear with colorful Seminole shirts. Sometimes designs are burned into leather or colored beads are used to decorate wide leather belts. "Ten-gallon" hats are worn more now than turbans. Some young Indians go bareheaded. Many dress like white men.

Seminoles of all ages like bright colors. A white great-grandmother would most likely dress in plain dark colors. An elderly Seminole woman might wear an ankle-length purple skirt with deeper purple orchids printed on it. Over this cloth, as a trimming, she might sew bands of colorful Seminole designs. With this she might wear a tent-like bright pink blouse bound tightly around the neck. Then she might put on strands and strands of many-colored beads, even if they are now out of style. She would feel properly dressed.

Chapter 23

The many groups of Seminoles have never been able to work close together as one strong nation. They are divided into family clans.

Florida Seminoles speak two separate languages. Most speak Mikasuki. Quite a number of all ages speak both Muskogee (Creek) and Mikasuki. The languages are so different that one group has trouble understanding the other group. Learning both languages helps. It is difficult to do because they have never been written.

These are a few Indian words in the English language: moccasin, succotash, chocolate, tobacco, tomato, hammock, and hurricane.

Any word in the Seminole language that ends in "ee" is connected to water.

Okeechobee means "Big Water."

Pahayokee means grassy water.

Kissimmee means winding water.

Wampee is a water plant (pickerel weed).

Hatchee means river.

Weeki Wachee means a small spring.

Many small towns on the middle west coast of Florida have Indian names.

Aripeka was named for a Seminole chief.

Elfers is Seminole for hunting grounds.

Wacasassa means cattle place.

Thonotosassa means flint place.

Chassahowitza means hanging pumpkin.

MikeSkeggs
88

Many Seminole children go to public schools or government schools. They know that they must read, write, and speak English if they intend to work in big cities when they grow up.

Florida has 67 counties. Nine of them bear Indian names. Most Seminoles today live in seven counties: Broward, Dade, Collier, Hendry, Glades, St. Lucie, and Okeechobee.

Many of them live on government reservations. There are three. Dania, in Broward County, is in the Fort Lauderdale-Miami area. Brighton, in Glades County, is northwest of Lake Okeechobee. Big Cypress, in Hendry County, is in the southern Everglades.

Each reservation now has a community building, a five-acre park, and a recreation area. The recreation buildings have furniture, TV sets, and games. Outside there is playground equipment. A director plans activities for children and grown people. Everybody can enjoy basketball, softball, baseball, and other games.

The Mikasuki Indians at first were very independent. They would not send their children to school. Now they are very proud of their basketball team.

Some still resent giving in to white men's ways, but many are gradually changing their way of thinking. At the close of the Seminole Wars, most of the Indians who refused to leave Florida and go to Oklahoma were Mikasuki. They went to live deep in the swamps of the Everglades. For many years white men hardly ever saw a Seminole. Then a few showed up at a trading post, about twenty years later. They had been living in small settlements on the few high points of land scattered widely through the Glades, or vast sawgrass country. Here they carried on hunting and trapping activities, almost completely apart from the rest of the world.

Until the 1930's schools and the Christian religion were almost unknown to them. They kept away from whites as much as possible. They had no desire to learn English. They kept away from tourist camps along the Tamiami Trail when the highway was first built.

Now "Trail Indians" help do road work, help white men harvest crops, drive trucks and tractors and work as parking lot attendants in Miami. Many sell frogs to large Miami hotels.

Two Seminole Tribal organizations have been formed in the last few years which have been helpful in bringing about progress. They are the Seminole Tribe of Florida and the Miccosukee Tribe of Indians of Florida. They are as stubbornly independent of one another as they have been of the United States. A number of people along the Tamiami Trail do not belong to either of these two tribal organizations.

Florida Seminoles can vote. They can become officers in the Florida State Government. They do not have to stay on a reservation. All are United States citizens.

Many are now attending schools, raising cattle, developing important housingprograms,and trying to adjust to the world of today.

Chapter 24

All Seminole children have a chance to get an education. Those in Head Start are learning to use a knife and fork. They are also learning English nursery rhymes and stories of such men as George Washington. Some older children go to high school at Miami.

Seminoles of Florida and Seminoles of Oklahoma are closely related. Many young Florida Seminoles go to high school and college today in Oklahoma.

Many who graduate from high school work to improve living conditions for their people. They hold important offices in the two Seminole tribal organizations. Some work at the Tribal Office and Agency. Several work at the Bureau of Indian Affairs in Washington, D.C.

Some older Seminoles think that Indian girls have too much freedom, that they should not go to school for very long because too much education makes them unhappy, that they should be trained to be good wives and mothers, should live in chickees instead of houses, and should learn to tan a deerskin. They believe that boys should be trained to do well the work for which they are best suited. They are not equipped for city competition. Boarding school teaches white man's culture. When Indians return to the reservations, they don't know how to survive. They can't skin a sheep, cook mutton, or cut wood.

Teachers for adults are on all three government reservations.

Indians own cattle ranches on the big reservations. They are being improved all of the time. Those who choose to work with cattle in the future will be doing a great service for their tribe.

By using new methods in drainage, irrigation, fertilization, and by using better quality grass and clover, they will improve their land. Without the new methods, twenty acres are needed to support one cow. Indians who change to new methods of land care find that one acre for each cow is enough.

Indian cowboys do their jobs well. Even through a hurricane they will stay with the cattle.

During the Seminole War, when troops marched back and forth across Indian country, burned villages, and destroyed crops, the Seminoles stopped building houses as they had once done. They decided that their homes would just be burned. They began to live in open shelters called chickees.

To build a chickee, first, four posts of cypress, pine, or palm were set in the ground. These poles held up the roof, which was a frame of cypress poles. Palmetto fronds were nailed close and thick to the cypress roof frame. Such a roofkept out the sun and rain.

Next, a floor was built about three feet above the ground to keep the chickee dry even in the rainy season. The low roof and open sides made the chickee comfortable in good weather. When the weather was bad, canvas or heavy material was used to close the sides. Benches were seats or tables by day and beds at night. Bed clothes were stored in rolls close under the roof.

If a chickee needed to be repaired, an Indian often built a new one instead of fixing the old one.

Seminoles still live in chickees, but as time goes on they begin to disappear. Some Indians are moving into modern homes on their reservations.

Often a large family built several chickees close together to make a camp. The family meant the father, mother, single children, and married daughters with their husbands. Any married son went to the home of his wife to live.

For those who live in this manner today, a special chickee is built in the middle of the camp. In this chickee a fire always burns on the ground. Eight or ten dry logs are arranged like spokes of a wheel. A fire burns at the center. As the logs burn, they are pushed toward the center. These logs make good seats near the fire at mealtime or in the evening.

Seminoles still eat the food their ancestors enjoyed. They like bear ribs, root jelly, hominy, corn cakes, and koonti. They stew or fry Florida fish, game, fruit and vegetables. Meals are usually a meat dish, bread, and rice served with a hot drink, especially in places where drinking water is unsafe.

Sofkee is cooked in huge black pots. It is mush made of ground corn, broth, fish, meat and vegetables added to make a good stew. Alligator tails, swamp cabbage – the white heart of the Sabal palm – make good additions, as well as turtle stew and black-eyed peas.

A large kettle of sofkee is always kept hot for all the people in the camp. Each family uses its own hand-carved white cypress spoon which leaves no taste in the drink or stew.

For snacks, plantains, swamp cabbage, and root of the dasheen are dipped in bowls of cane syrup or hot bacon drippings.

Indians eat whenever they get hungry, sometimes twice a day, sometimes less. There is plenty. For years they had no refrigerators. It became the custom to cook only enough for a meal and eat all the food.

Long ago it was a custom to have feasts at every celebration, but that has changed. Feasts at cattle round-ups or to celebrate birthdays of important people of the tribe are still popular.

In days past, a family of several generations lived in a camp of chickees around a cooking and dining area used by all. Some still do.

A scene such as this might be found in a Mikasuki village deep in the Everglades. Melons, pumpkins, and corn may be growing near the chickee.

A baby is sleeping in a hammock that hangs high in a chickee. A little girl is playing with a doll made from the bud of a palm tree. An older daughter is grinding corn in a hollowed log. To crush the corn, she is using a wooden pestle. Some day she hopes to use a hand-cranked corn grinder, as many Seminoles now do. A turtle roasts in his shell on his back on a bed of hot coals.

The mother is doing the family wash. She works at the edge of the brown water. Juices from the cypress roots color it that way. She dips clothes in the brown water, pounds them on a rock, and rinses them in the water. She spreads them on the bushes in the hot sun to dry. She uses no soap, bleach or starch.

Some parents live in chickee camps. Their married children may live on a reservation or in a new house. Some older folks who like chickees have electricity for an iron, a hand-turned sewing machine and a TV set. They cook outside over an open fire and sleep in an open chickee with only mosquito nets for protection.

Some build chickees near a daughter's new home. They may or may not use the kitchen and bath. Some house owners continue to cook and eat outdoors.

New homes use part chickee and part modern white man's ideas. The outside may be unpainted cypress with a thatched-palm-frond-covered roof. Under the thatch, the roof will be solid. The building will be open to the breeze by means of screens above partial walls. These screens may be covered with sheets of plastic. Some homes have sliding windows.

Houses have indoor kitchens and bathrooms. Stucco, concrete block, heat, and insulation are not used. Electric stoves, refrigerators, sewing machines, and TV sets are installed.

Indians do most of the building.

Big Cypress Reservation has a group of these new homes. Some have two or three bedrooms. Most have electricity, washing machines, refrigerators, sewing machines, radios, and television sets. There are street lights, paved streets, and sidewalks.

It is not unusual to see a chickee in a yard. Sometimes parents or grandparents want to live close to younger members of their families but do not feel comfortable in new modern homes.

All reservations today have churches and Indian ministers.

Chapter 25

M Seminoles have adopted many ways of white men and have changed some of their own. Some refuse to give up their customs and laws handed down to them by ancestors long ago.

Once they were driven from their land of game, fish, and freedom to live as they wished in middle Florida. They fled to the mosquito-infested watery wilderness of the Everglades to build an entirely new life for themselves. The unkind soil and unkind climate were no help, but they were determined to live in Florida.

They are accustomed to this way of living and like it. They do not want their children to change, but the Everglades are changing.

Parts of the swamps are being drained for farming. Trees are being cut for lumber. Game animals are disappearing. White men are again invading their lands. Forest fires, dry weather, floods, and hurricanes are causing destruction. Many young Seminoles are leaving. An Indian cannot make a good living today by hunting.

Today each Indian must choose the way that is best for him. Most older Seminoles want to keep apart from white men. Many want to work with white men and live as they do. Most of the younger people want to go to school and learn to speak good English. They can do this as well as keep customs of the tribe. They need not stop practice of their own language, songs, and dances.

Indians work well with tools, are good in sports, and are busier than ever on the reservations. They own horses, hogs, and chickens. Some work on vegetable farms, build roads, drive trucks and tractors, work on parking lots, and help at lumber mills near their homes. Still others work at camps along highways.

Men wrestle alligators or trim cypress logs for dugouts while tourists watch. Women make bright colored clothes to sell. Almost every home has a sewing machine of some kind. Electric sewing machines are rapidly replacing hand-turned machines. Seminole women can not sew fast enough on the small hand-turned machines to supply the tourists.

Chapter 26

Hunting and trapping once were the only ways Seminoles had to support themselves. Otter, skunk, coon, and alligator hides were easy to sell. Alligator hunters were called skin hunters. These hunters traveled deep into the Everglades in their dugouts. They hunted at night with torches or lanterns. Alligators came close to the bright lights, where they were easily shot. As many as a thousand were killed in one lake.

Today a law forbids the killing of alligators as they are considered an endangered species. They dig water holes. During the dry season these holes are about the only places where wild animals and birds can get water. Since water is being drained from parts of the Everglades for more farmland, wild life is suffering.

Long ago hunters skinned the alligators and salted the hides, which they carried for miles through swamps and over bad trails to white traders. The Indians traded hides for ammunition, cloth, or money. If they chose money, they were given less than seventy cents for each hide.

Seminoles make excellent tourist guides. They are still fine hunters. They hunt deer, bears, wild hogs, wild ducks, opossums, turtles, and frogs. They are good fishermen, too. They especially like gar and catfish.

For their work some Indians use air boats. An airplane propeller at the back and on the top of a boat makes it speed through water and saw-grass without danger of entangling the propeller with the weeds.

Some day children will have to make a big decision. Will they choose white men's ways? Will they remain in the swampland where they'll never know about ice cream, bubble gum, and the many more-important things of the white man's civilization? At present they do not have much time to play or think. There are pigs under the chickee floor to be fed. There is wood to be carried or a young brother or sister to watch.

When they're young, they learn that they must work. Before they are much older, they will learn to be quiet, like their parents, when white men are present.

Today they play with white children's toys. Their parents played with seashells or dry seed pods, from jungle trees, that rattled when they were shaken.

Children are not the only Indians who must make decisions. There are the Indians who served well in our World Wars. They were active in carrying secret messages. Two Indians could speak freely without the enemy understanding what they said.

When they came home, their places in their own villages were gone and they had no part in the white American community. Indian heroes were forced to choose between tribe and white people.

Chapter 27

Indians have no absolute ruler. In the past, a council of older men often chose one of their members as a leader. Generally each small band did this.

The government for many years has tried to get the Seminoles to live like white men. A chief who worked with the government was not always recognized as such by his tribe.

Tribes do not think and plan alike. For that reason it is almost impossible to choose one leader.

An Indian worker must feel that he is working for himself and for his own tribe. He has no use for time clocks, for management other than the tribe itself, or for regular working hours.

He may wish to work around the clock or not for a week. He may wish to work at home with his family or just fish and hunt. At the end of the month he will accept a pay check for work he has done. All his life he had been accustomed to free sharing.

The government had been taking care of the Indians. Then it was decided to teach them farming, give them farms, and make them citizens. Such a plan didn't last long, because white men soon had possession of their farms. These white men then demanded that the government take care of the Indians as it had been doing.

Next the government encouraged Indians to farm government-held land managed by an overseer. This stopped white men from taking land from the Indians and brought tribes closer together.

White men demanded that reservation size be cut. Disease, poor food and hopelessness for the future discouraged young men and even made some commit suicide.

White conquerors changed Indian religious beliefs, territory, way of life, and means of existence.

No one will ever know how many Indians of how many tribes were made slaves, tortured, and killed. The homes, dignity, culture, great accomplishments, and freedom of hundreds of people were destroyed.

When an overseer or agent, sent by the United States Government at Washington, D.C., took charge of a reservation, he was given all kinds of power. He could put Indians in prison, sentence them, break up families, take children from parents, and decide where an Indian should live and how he should spend his time.

For the most part, he just kept Indians on a reservation. He stopped them from killing each other and white officers. He hired a few Indians who could speak English. They became interpreters and clerks. He could keep Indian policemen and appoint a few judges. If he didn't like their decisions, he could settle troubles himself.

The government provided food, clothes, and tools for the Indians. The agent gave these to people as they were needed. He bought train-loads of cattle to help Indians get started in the cattle business. He hired Indian labor to build roads on the reservation.

A few white men opened stores at the agency and sold all kinds of goods. Indians who worked at the agency paid very high prices for anything they bought.

Some white families lived near the agency. Sometimes there was a doctor or a missionary.

Leaders of the tribe felt that the agency wasn't fair. Young Indians threatened trouble but were asked by the tribe not to complain. Sometimes the young couldn't be trusted. Agents had to be brave and think fast sometimes to save their own lives.

The government wanted Indians to live in log or wooden

houses instead of shelters. Indians were asked to wear "citizen's dress," put money in the bank, begin to farm at once and cut their hair. Agents tried to carry out the wishes of the government. They refused to employ Indians who didn't cut their hair. So many Indians who tried to live in log or wooden houses got sick that they went back to their former shelters.

Indian farmers were supposed to succeed as well as white farmers. They had no money to back them up. One very big drawback was their belief that one person couldn't own land. It belonged to everybody. All should share alike.

They were told to begin to raise "civilized crops" – not beans, squashes, and maize. This insulted hunting tribes. They said that farming was women's work.

The agent listened to their complaints but did nothing.

The little group that fled to the swamps lived like hunted animals. They were ready to flee at a moment's notice and ready to fight to the death if necessary.

They listened to the advice of an old medicine man: "Grow like the corn. Put your roots down deeply. Then you will be able to sway in the winds of trouble and change, but the roots will not let you be blown away from your home."

That fierce, proud, independent group listened and prospered.

Although Indians are divided in their views about uniting tribes, some progress has been made. Before too many years one strong central government for all Seminoles may be established, as these people feel that they are citizens of Florida and of the United States. Since the U.S. Government paid $16 million to settle Seminole claims, the sense of belonging may be strengthened.

Mike Skaggs

GLOSSARY

– A –

aboriginal – earliest known inhabitants of Florida

Ais – at one time the most important tribe on the southeastern Florida coast. Their village was located on the lagoon which is known as Indian River, a section of the Intercoastal Waterway. The strong Calusa controlled them.

Apalachee – a large tribe known for their courage in fighting. They were good farmers and fine workers.

Apalachen – forty dirty, deserted low thatched huts which stood on the shore of Lake Miccosukee. Some corn and dried fish were the jewels found by Narvaez in this "great city of riches," as pictured by the Indians.

Apalachicola – a Muskogean Indian of northwestern Florida

Aucilla – a river in northern Florida

atlatl – spear-thrower

– B –

Bimini – an island where the "fountain of youth" was supposed to be located. According to legend, the island was constructed of almost pure gold – not coral, sand, and palms.

bodkin – a sharp, pointed instrument of bone used for making holes; sometimes it is a kind of pin used by women for fastening the hair.

breechclout – sometimes called breech-cloth. It is a piece of cloth or leather worn about the hips by primitive man. Some breechclouts were worn with fringed sashes. Some sashes were bordered with tassels.

– C –

cacique – Indian chief

Calusa – unusual prehistoric artists. Their spear-throwers were beautifully carved. Spears and clubs had shark teeth glued into slots in exact rows. They made tools of antlers, shark teeth, fish jaws, bones, shells, and coral, which were often decorated and carved. Shell pendants and earrings were inlaid and colored. Wooden jewelry was inlaid with tortoise shell. Some carved animal heads had ears that moved. They were attached with leather. Wild animals were painted on wood. Cushions for furniture were made of woven mats. These people were fierce fighters and daring seamen. They traveled to Cuba and other islands of the Caribbean Sea. They owned many scattered towns. Perhaps Tampa was the most northern.

Canaveral – Spanish word that means a place of reeds or cane

chickees – open shelters; four posts hold up a low, palmetto-covered roof; the floor is about three feet above the ground; sides are open in good weather and closed with heavy curtains in bad weather.

chunky – from "chungke," name of a game formerly played by Creeks in a square area surrounded by a bank. The area was used for ceremonials and games. Players throw or slide a pole so that a crook at one end curves around a disk.

coontie – The Seminole term for white root or white bread is "conti hatcka"; from this comes the more common name, "coontie." It is the cooked, fleshy rootstock which was used by Florida Indians as an important food source. [This information was taken from *A Flora of Tropical Florida,* a manual of the seed plants and ferns of Southern Peninsular Florida. Copyright, 1971, University of Miami Press, by Robert W. Long, Ph.D., Professor of Botany, University of South Florida; and Olga Lakela, Ph.D., Research Associate in Botany, University of South Florida.]

Creek – An American Indian of northwestern Florida

culture – Culture is the way of life as it is lived by a tribe or group of related tribes in the same stage of development or advancement. Common interests in education, training, improvement of manners and tastes build toward greater achievement by future generations.

– D –

dasheen – a root that has food value similar to a potato; it is grown throughout Florida.

dredged – deepened, such as the deepening of a water-course

– E –

embers – coals, burning and smoking without flame among ashes remaining from a fire *epidemic* – a widely-spread disease which attacks many people at the same time

Everglades – a large tract of marshland in Southern Florida

– F –

fiber – a slender root such as grass

flint point – stone point

flounder – struggle or splash through mud and water

Fountain of Youth – ancient Indian legend beginning in the West Indies concerning fountain which would maintain or rekindle youth in a person

fragrant – pleasant-smelling, such as the odor of a perfume

frigid – very cold

frond – leaf of a palm

– G –

gorget – a piece of armor protecting the throat. Sometimes a gorget was made of stone, bone, or shell, and was probably also used as a neck or breast ornament.

gourds – related to the squash and pumpkin family; dried shells of the fruit were used as dippers or other utensils.

– H –

hammocks – scrub, pineland

hemp – tough fiber of a plant used for making cloth and rope

hummock – slight rise of fertile ground above a level surface; island of dense tropical undergrowth in the Everglades

– I –

infested – troubled by great numbers

interpreter – one who explains the meaning of a different language

– K –

kite – a bird of the hawk family with long, narrow wings and deeply-forked tail, noted for its graceful and sustained flight

– L –

lightwood – a dry wood that burns readily – kindling wood

limpkin – a large, brown, wading bird

litter – a couch with poles at the sides, often provided with curtains. It was used for carrying a chief or other important persons.

— M —

manatee — a tropical, aquatic mammal, about 10 feet long, found along Florida coasts

mango — evergreen tree grown in tropics, with large, delicious fruit

mangrove — a tropical, evergreen tree or shrub

moat — a deep and wide ditch usually filled with water, usually placed around a town as protection against the enemy

moccasin — shoe of the American Indians made of deerskin or other soft leather. The sole and upper are in one piece.

mortar — a strong vessel in which food or other substances were pounded or rubbed to break them down

— O —

obligated — bound by duty or a promise

obsidian — a shiny black or very dark-colored stone that splinters easily; it was used by primitive people in the manufacture of knives or other implements.

opponent — one who is on the opposite side of a contest

overseer — a supervisor or superintendent of workmen in their labor

— P —

partial — part, not all

peninsula — land nearly surrounded by water

Pensacola — a word meaning "hair people." Both men and women wore their hair long. This was a small and unimportant group driven from their territory by warriors of other tribes. They nearly killed Narvaez. With some of his officers, Narvaez had accepted an invitation to spend the night in the house of the chief. Indians made a surprise attack after midnight when all were asleep. Narvaez was struck in the head with a stone and knocked unconscious. Some Spanish soldiers carried him to his boat. Indians were overcome, and Spaniards slipped away in the darkness.

pestle — club-shaped implement for grinding or pounding food or other substances in a mortar

— Q —

quiver — case for carrying arrows

– R –

reeds – tall grass with slender, often jointed stems

roseate spoonbill – a wading bird with chiefly pink feathers. Its bill is wide and flattened at the tip.

Royal Poinciana – a tropical tree with scarlet and orange flowers. It also has flat seed pods sometimes 2 feet in length.

rushes – plants often having round, hollow stems that grow in soft, wet land. They were used by the Indians in braiding mats.

– S –

shaft – the long handle of a spear or the stem of an arrow

shaman – a medicine man who is believed to have contact with the unseen world of gods and spirits of ancestors. He is said to have the power to cure the sick and drive off evil spirits.

shards – (sometimes called "sherds") – pieces of a broken earthen vessel

sinews – tough, strong bands or cords of animal tissue

sloth – a slow-moving animal that hangs from tree branches, back-downward, and feeds entirely on leaves, shoots, and fruits

soffkee – thin mush made of cornmeal

Spanish bayonet – a stiff, short-trunked plant of the southern United States with rigid, spine-tipped leaves

Spanish moss – a plant that grows on another plant and derives its moisture and food from air and rain, with grayish-green strands on branches of trees in the southern United States

spiral – winding or circling round a center and gradually receding from it

stucco – outside coating for walls in which cement is largely used

succotash – beans and fresh grains of Indian corn, often with pieces of salt pork added

– T –

tapered – becoming gradually smaller toward one end

Tequesta – Sometimes called "Takesta" (used by J. U. Terrell – authoritative reference and chronicle, *American Indian Almanac,* Crowell Co. 1971). The Takesta were the earliest known people to live on the site of the city of Miami. They were ruled by the stronger Calusa.

thongs – leather straps or strips used for fastening a moccasin

Timucua – An Indian tribe scattered over northern Florida, from south of Cape Canaveral to Georgia and from Tampa Bay to the Aucilla River. They did much to drive Ponce de Leon from Florida. Men and women tattooed their bodies. Although tribes were scattered, they were well organized to fight together. It may be they were the first Indians to tell Narvaez that a city far to the north was rich in jewels.

Timucuan – a tentative language family comprising only the Timucua language and perhaps related to Muskogean

Tocobaga – another Florida Indian tribe which lived during the time Spain ruled

– U –

utensils – vessels or other articles used in a household, especially the kitchen

– V –

violating – breaking or disregarding

– W –

Withlacoochie – Indian meaning – little great river, named by the Creek Indians for a river of the same name near their home in Georgia. It is a swift-flowing, rock-bottomed stream, very deep where Narvaez tried to cross.